After-School FUN

Bike Riding

by JoAnn Early Macken

Reading consultant: Susan Nations, M.Ed., author/literacy coach/consultant

Please visit our web site at: www.earlyliteracy.cc
For a free color catalog describing Weekly Reader® Early Learning Library's list of high-quality books, call 1-877-445-5824 (USA) or 1-800-387-3178 (Canada). Weekly Reader® Early Learning Library's fax: (414) 336-0164.

Library of Congress Cataloging-in-Publication Data

Macken, JoAnn Early, 1953-
Bike riding / by JoAnn Early Macken.
p. cm. — (After-school fun)
Includes bibliographical references and index.
ISBN 0-8368-4512-9 (lib. bdg.)
ISBN 0-8368-4519-6 (softcover)
1. Cycling—Juvenile literature. I. Title.
GV1043.5.M32 2005
796.6—dc22 2004059704

This edition first published in 2005 by
Weekly Reader® Early Learning Library
330 West Olive Street, Suite 100
Milwaukee, WI 53212 USA

Photographer: Gregg Andersen
Picture research: Diane Laska-Swanke
Art direction and page layout: Tammy West

Printed in the United States of America

1 2 3 4 5 6 7 8 9 09 08 07 06 05

Note to Educators and Parents

Reading is such an exciting adventure for young children! They are beginning to integrate their oral language skills with written language. To encourage children along the path to early literacy, books must be colorful, engaging, and interesting; they should invite the young reader to explore both the print and the pictures.

After-School Fun is a new series designed to help children read about the kinds of activities they enjoy in their free time. In each book, young readers learn about a different artistic endeavor, physical activity, or learning experience.

Each book is specially designed to support the young reader in the reading process. The familiar topics are appealing to young children and invite them to read — and reread — again and again. The full-color photographs and enhanced text further support the student during the reading process.

In addition to serving as wonderful picture books in schools, libraries, homes, and other places where children learn to love reading, these books are specifically intended to be read within an instructional guided reading group. This small group setting allows beginning readers to work with a fluent adult model as they make meaning from the text. After children develop fluency with the text and content, the book can be read independently. Children and adults alike will find these books supportive, engaging, and fun!

— Susan Nations, M.Ed., author, literacy coach,
and consultant in literacy development

After school, I unlock my bike. I put on my helmet. My helmet helps protect my head. Now I can go for a ride!

BELL

My friends ride bikes, too. We ride our bikes on the playground. We ride in big circles on the playground.

My friend's bike has training wheels. Training wheels help keep his bike steady. Soon, he will be able to ride without them.

Dad comes to meet me. My sister comes, too. Dad's bike is bigger than mine. My sister's bike is smaller.

FRANKLIN
SCHOOL
18
Raleigh

A tricycle has three wheels. When I was little, I rode a tricycle. Now my sister rides it.

Little People
SCHOOL BUS

We ride home from school. I ride on the sidewalk. My sister does, too. The sidewalk is safer for kids.

We stop at the corner. We look both ways for cars. Dad tells us when it is safe to cross the street.

NO
PARKING
18
GIANT

On nice days, we ride on the bike path. We see trees and flowers. We hear birds sing.

NO
MOTORIZED
VEHICLES
PERMITTED

I like to be outside. I like to feel the wind in my face. I like to ride fast on the bike path!

Glossary

training wheels — a pair of small wheels on the back of a bike that help the rider balance

tricycle — a vehicle with three wheels

unlock — to open a lock

For More Information

Books

Bicycle Book. Gail Gibbons (Holiday House)

Bicycles. Transportation Library (series). Lola M. Schaefer (Bridgestone)

Ethan's Bike. Brand New Readers (series). Johanna Hurwitz (Candlewick Press)

Play It Safe. Skills and Practice (series). Mercer Mayer (McGraw-Hill)

Web Sites

Propelled by Pedals: A Fun Guide to Bikes!
library.thinkquest.org/J002670/
Bicycle history, stunts, safety tips, jokes, poems

Index

About the Author

JoAnn Early Macken is the author of two rhyming picture books, *Sing-Along Song* and *Cats on Judy*, and six other series of nonfiction books for beginning readers. Her poems have appeared in several children's magazines. A graduate of the M.F.A. in Writing for Children and Young Adults program at Vermont College, she lives in Wisconsin with her husband and their two sons. Visit her Web site at www.joannmacken.com.